Where Does a Graph Go?

BY JOY VISTO

CREATIVE EDUCATION

CREATIVE PAPERBACKS

Published by Creative Education and Creative Paperbacks
P.O. Box 227, Mankato, Minnesota 56002
Creative Education and Creative Paperbacks
are imprints of The Creative Company
www.thecreativecompany.us

Design and production by Liddy Walseth
Art direction by Rita Marshall
Printed in the United States of America

Photographs by Dreamstime (Julvil, Rangizzz), Getty Images (Oppenheim Bernhard,
Peter Cade, Patrik Giardino, Imagno, Joan Vicent Cantó Roig),
iStockphoto (4x6, Andyd, Antagain, franckreporter, GeoffBlack, Grafissimo, JoeFotoIS,
magnetcreative, marekuliasz, OSTILL, studiocasper, Tomwang112, ValentynVolkov,
yenisanat, yganko, yumiyum, ZU_09), Shutterstock (Arkady Mazor, Vitalinka, Yganko)
Vector illustrations by Donny Gettinger

Library of Congress Cataloging-in-Publication Data
Visto, Joy.
Where does a graph go? / Joy Visto.
p. cm. — (Making math work)
Includes bibliographical references and index.
Summary: A helpful guide for understanding the mathematical concepts and real-world
applications of graphs and diagrams, including classroom tips, common terms such as
variables, and exercises to encourage hands-on practice.
ISBN 978-1-60818-575-7 (hardcover)
ISBN 978-1-62832-176-0 (pbk)
1. Graphic methods—Juvenile literature. 2. Mathematics—Graphic methods—Juvenile
literature. 3. Mathematics—Charts, diagrams, etc.—Juvenile literature. I. Title.

QA90.V567 2015
511.5—dc23 2014034839

CCSS: RI.5.1, 2, 3, 8; RI.6.1, 2, 3, 4, 5, 6, 7; RST.6-8.3, 4, 6, 7

First Edition HC 9 8 7 6 5 4 3 2 1
First Edition PBK 9 8 7 6 5 4 3 2 1

When you think about mathematics, you probably think about a class at school where you do **calculations** and answer word problems. But have you ever thought about math being all around you? It's in every shape and pattern you see. It's in every song you hear. It's in every game you play and any puzzle you solve! The first mathematicians realized this, and they looked for ways to prove it—to show how order and reason could explain much about life as they knew it. Sometimes this was easy to do. But other times, people just didn't get it. Even some of the most intelligent people in history have struggled with math: Albert Einstein once wrote to a child, "Do not worry about your difficulties in Mathematics. I can assure you mine are still greater."

So how can you use whatever you know about math in everyday life? When you explain your *location* to a friend who is meeting you at the mall, make a *substitution* with another player in a basketball game, or watch the *path* of a ball flying through the air, you are using math! These ideas are important in a branch of math known as algebraic **geometry**. Algebraic geometry is concerned with drawing graphs of different **equations** so that they can be studied. *Where does* this branch of math show up in your own life?

Prominent American Series

ALBERT EINSTEIN 8c
MATHEMATICIAN – PHYSICIST
NOBEL PRIZE WINNER
1879 – 1955
Artmaster

First Day of Issue

THE LINES MADE BY ROADS ON A MAP FORM A MATHEMATICAL-LOOKING GRID.

COMMON LOCATORS

MUCH OF THE MATHEMATICS THAT YOU DO INVOLVES WORKING WITH A ONE-DIMENSIONAL SET OF NUMBERS. Even when you add two numbers together, the final sum is just one number. The same holds true for the other **operations** that you do. The result will always be another number. You are essentially just moving forward and backward on a giant number line. The numbers that you calculate with can be considered points on a number line.

This idea expands as you get into a **two-dimensional** space. One of the main principles of geometry is that two points make up a line. You may also know that two points can be used for graphing in algebra, but it wasn't always that way. Mathematicians were able to argue ideas in geometry and solve problems with algebra, but the two branches didn't come together until the early 17th century.

Think of those two points in space as being two cities. The road connecting those two cities can be thought of as a line. If you travel between the cities, you are traveling on that line. If you stay on that road to go to another city, you are still just traveling in one dimension. Essentially, you're moving along a number line by doing calculations. But what happens if you want to go to a city that isn't on the same road?

In real life, you can use a map

to represent all the different cities as points. Mathematicians would call those points loci, or groups of points that follow a specific rule. Always looking for ways to apply their knowledge in daily life, mathematicians realized they needed a more general way of discussing things such as loci.

Loci are a way to talk about geometric figures with more algebraic rules. How would you describe a circle to a friend? Would you say it is a shape that doesn't have any corners? That's a great description, and your friend would probably be able to picture a circle. However, a mathematician would describe a circle as the set of all points that are the same distance from a given point. Describing it like that is talking about a circle as a locus. Prior to the development of the **coordinate plane**, though, that was difficult.

It was also difficult to pinpoint specific points within loci without having a system for naming or identifying their positions. Think about it this way: If someone wanted to leave a note on your desk at school but had never been inside your classroom, how would you explain the location to them? You would need to use terms that have meaning to both of you. You couldn't just say, "two in from the right in the first row." Depending on which direction you're facing, that could mean different things! You need an origin point to reference, like the teacher's desk or the door. From that origin point, it becomes easier to describe the locations of other objects in the room. You also need common axes (or straight, fixed

PTOLEMY'S *GEOGRAPHY* MAPPED THE PLACES KNOWN TO FIRST-CENTURY ROMANS.

𝔓𝔱𝔬𝔩𝔢𝔪𝔞𝔬𝔰 1. 𝔏𝔞𝔤𝔬𝔰

lines) to talk about, such as rows and columns of desks. French philosopher and mathematician Rene Descartes tackled this topic of loci, origin points, and axes. When Descartes was a little boy, he had some health issues that kept him in bed until 11:00 each morning. He ended up making a habit of late rising throughout his life. It is said that while lying in bed one day, Descartes noticed a fly on his ceiling. He began to wonder how he might be able to tell a friend about this fly's position as well as track the fly's movements. Legend has it that from this experience, Descartes developed the system that now bears his name—the Cartesian coordinate plane.

The coordinate plane is now a common system for explaining locations in two-dimensional space. Ancient civilizations, such as the Greeks, had used a rectangular grid system for dividing and mapping particular areas. For example, around the year 100, Claudius Ptolemy proposed using such a system for mapping specific regions. Other civilizations used similar methods as they constructed maps for navigation, exploration, and trade. However, these civilizations did not have a method common to each other, which is what the Cartesian plane gave mathematicians 1,500 years later.

Descartes generated his coordinate plane by unknowingly following in the footsteps of fellow French mathematician Pierre de Fermat. Fermat, whose everyday job was practicing law, is most commonly associated with **number theory**. He postulated, or proposed, an idea about the relationship of **powers** of numbers that remained unproven for approximately

You need an
ORIGIN POINT
to reference

350 years. This idea is known as Fermat's Last Theorem.

However, one of Fermat's other contributions to math was his early development of the coordinate plane. Fermat became interested in solving problems with loci, following the work of the Greek mathematician Apollonius. Apollonius studied different curves as they appeared in geometry. Fermat extended this work by investigating relationships between two **variables**. He assigned the letter A to the x-variable and the letter E to the y-variable. Fermat started by drawing a horizontal line whose length was A. He then drew another line with length E. He did not have a standard angle for the intersection of A and E that was the same for every graph, but within each graph that angle was the same. He plotted his points at the end of this second segment. These points represented the relationship between A and E. Because much of Fermat's mathematical work was never published, people did not learn about it until later.

As a result, Descartes developed his system independently. Like Fermat, Descartes started his system by putting the x-variable on the

THE TWO MAIN AXES CAN BE USED TO GRAPH OPEN CURVES CALLED HYPERBOLAS.

horizontal axis. He then represented the y-variable along a second axis. (With the coordinate plane you use now, the y-variable is represented on a vertical axis.) Descartes, like Fermat, believed that the angle between *x* and *y* did not matter. Both plotted points by treating the values of *x* and *y* as line segments to travel along. At the time, it was common to treat numbers as lengths of segments rather than abstract quantities representing amounts.

Over the years, the Cartesian plane became what you now know and recognize. The x-axis and y-axis intersect, or cross, at the origin point and form a perfect 90-degree angle. This angle was implemented by English mathematician and physicist Isaac Newton at the turn of the 18th century. As the axes developed, so did the math for which they were used.

Plotting points on the coordinate plane generates different types of lines and curves. Those lines can be used to examine how

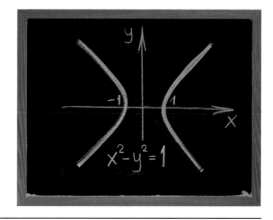

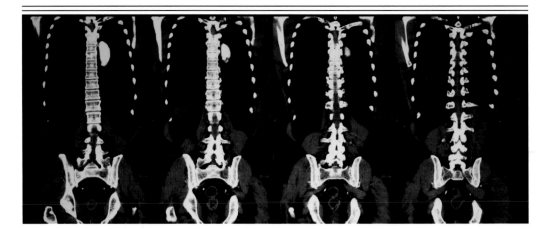

All the slices together
FORM MANY
coordinate planes

two variables are related or unrelated. Mathematicians soon needed to
be able to examine relationships among more than two variables. As
the years went on, a third axis was added. This axis, the z-axis, is used
for representing three-dimensional situations.

Many developments in fields other than mathematics have come as
a direct result of the work on coordinate planes. For example, in hospi-
tals, in order to diagnose a patient, doctors can order a CAT scan. This
type of X-ray takes pictures of the body in slices and then pieces those
slices together to give doctors a three-dimensional view of what is happening inside the body. Each individual slice is made up of information
that has been plotted on a coordinate plane. All the slices together form
many coordinate planes.

While generating pictures of the human body is a specific applica-
tion for the coordinate plane, you probably know it better as a way to
plot points so that you can draw lines and other curves. Not only can
you tell a friend where your desk is, but you can also draw a line to your
friend's desk in the coordinate plane of your classroom. And all this
started by watching a fly on the ceiling!

Think Like Descartes

While mathematicians celebrate Descartes for his work in uniting algebra and geometry, he is probably best known for his philosophical trail-blazing. He chose to accept only the things that he knew for certain, such as the fact that he existed. From this process, he coined the phrase, "Cogito, ergo sum," which means "I think, therefore I am." Descartes believed that he existed to think, and that through thinking, he was able to exist.

PUTTING POINTS ON PAPER

THE CHIEF BENEFIT OF THE COORDINATE PLANE WAS THE ABILITY TO HAVE A COMMON SYSTEM FOR WORKING WITH LOCATION. Mathematicians were now able to give the location of a point based on two distances. But in order to communicate such locations to others, they needed a common language as well. So, the concept of ordered pairs was developed. Ordered pairs are just a list of two quantities. You probably recognize them in this form: (*x*, *y*), which tells you how to plot points on a graph.

Before Descartes, mathematicians were not using letters for variables. Instead, they used the words *cosa* or *coss*, which both mean "thing." In the 1500s, though, François Viète first proposed the use of letters in calculations. His plan was to use vowels (a, e, i, o, and u) as variables, or unknown quantities. The remaining letters, the consonants, would be used as known quantities. Descartes modified that idea by choosing the letters *x* and *y* to represent unknown quantities. The letters at the beginning of the alphabet were re-

X-VALUE
Y-VALUE

served for known quantities called constants.

X and y can be mapped to dimensions on the coordinate plane. The x-value tells how to travel along the horizontal axis of the graph. The y-value tells how to travel along the vertical axis of the graph. Positive numbers represent moving right or up, and negative numbers represent moving left or down. Every point starts at (0, 0), the origin point, or the place where the two axes intersect. Take a look at the ordered pairs listed below. Follow along with the directions provided, and notice that whenever a point is plotted, it is labeled with a letter.

A (2, 3): Move two units to the right of the origin. From that place, move up three units.
B (-4, 7): Move four units to the left of the origin. From that place, move up seven units.
C (-3, -1): Move three units to the left of the origin. From that place, move down one unit.
D (5, -4): Move five units to the right of the origin. From that place, move down four units.

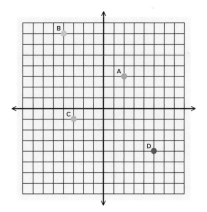

It's your turn to try and plot the following points. Remember to always start from the origin!

E (1, 6)   F (-2, -2)   G (-5, 3)   H (6, -2) *

*Answer Key: Problem A

You may have noticed that the signs of each ordered pair tell something about where the point will be plotted. Every coordinate plane can be divided into four quadrants, or sections, by the two axes. Points in a given quadrant have the same signs on their x- and y-values.

If both the x-value and the y-value are positive, the point will be in the top-right quadrant. This is called the first quadrant. If the x-value is negative but the y-value is positive, then the point will be in the top-left, second quadrant. For ordered pairs whose values are both negative, their points are located in the bottom-left corner. This area is the third quadrant. The fourth quadrant is the lower-right corner, where the x-value is positive and the y-value is negative. If there is a zero in the ordered pair, the point does not lie in a quadrant but instead can be found on an axis.

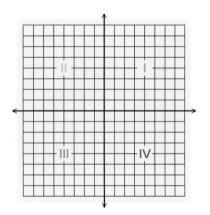

If you know where each point is supposed to be located, it will help you plot it. Before you get started, determine in which quadrant they belong. When it comes time to plot them, you should check to see whether the point is where you predicted it would be. Try this as you plot the following points.

J (4, -3)   K (-1, 7)   L (-6, -5)   M (0, 3) *

In addition to plotting ordered pairs that someone else comes up with, you can generate your own from a given equation. Ordered pairs are great for representing locations, but *x* and *y* can stand for more than just numbers in a coordinate plane.

*Answer Key: Problem B

Determine in WHICH QUADRANT they belong

These variables can also be used to represent the relationship between the input and output of a specific rule. These rules can be used to calculate a variety of quantities, including length, area, or volume. The values used for *x* are the inputs. This group of numbers is a set called the domain. The outputs, or y-values, are a set of numbers known as the range. Pairs of inputs and outputs are known as a relation. A more specific type of relation is a function. A function is a relation in which every input has only one output.

You can see how relations and functions work by looking at a cell phone. Some cell phones use a type of keypad called T9, or text on nine keys. In this form, the input of the 2 button gives an output of the letters *A*, *B*, and *C*. Because there is more than one output for the input, this system of typing is like a relation. As cell phones evolved, they began to use a QWERTY layout, like the keyboard of a computer. In that layout, the 2 button outputs only a 2. The input has only one output. A keyboard like this represents a function.

PHONES WITH A T9 KEYBOARD RESULT IN MULTIPLE OUTPUTS FOR EACH INPUT.

Using the equations that represent most functions, you can make your own ordered pairs. This is done using substitution—the process of replacing an unknown quantity with a known number. If you substitute a value for *x*, you are inputting a number into your function and adding a number to the domain. The answer you get when calculating for *y* is an output value, a number in the range. Together, the two numbers yield an ordered pair.

In the following example, you need to generate a list of five ordered pairs using the function y = 3x + 5. For a domain, you can use any values of *x* that you would like. For starters, let's use 1, 2, 3, and 4. Begin by replacing the *x* in the equation with each number. After that, follow the order of operations to finish calculating. The **acronym** PEMDAS gives the proper order for performing operations: parentheses, exponents, multiplication, division, addition, and subtraction. All calculations are performed in order from left to right, just as you are reading the sentences in this book.

YOU CAN TELL A QWERTY KEYBOARD BY THE FIRST SIX LETTERS ON ITS TOP ROW.

y = 3x + 5	y = 3x + 5	y = 3x + 5	y = 3x + 5
y = 3(1) + 5	y = 3(2) + 5	y = 3(3) + 5	y = 3(4) + 5
y = 3 + 5	y = 6 + 5	y = 9 + 5	y = 12 + 5
y = 8	y = 11	y = 14	y = 17

The ordered pairs from these four equations are (1,8), (2,11), (3,14), and (4,17). You can plot those on a graph. Using the same method, try to find four ordered pairs from the following equations.

$$y = 2x + 7 \qquad\qquad y = 5x - 2 \qquad\qquad y = -4x + 6 \quad *$$

Now that you have generated some ordered pairs, plot them on a graph. What shape do they begin to resemble? They should start to form a line.

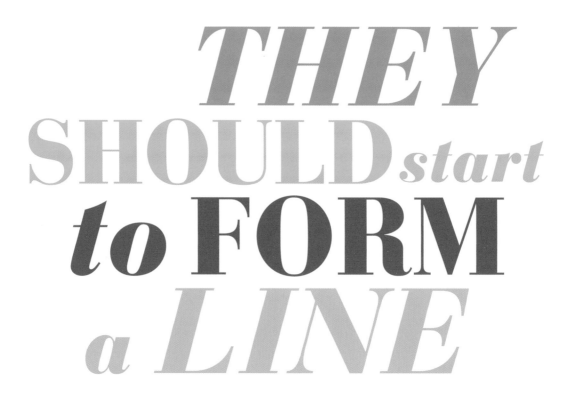

THEY
SHOULD *start*
to FORM
a LINE

Answer Key: Problem C

Z Equals 3-D

When the three-dimensional z-axis is put in play, the coordinate plane has to change. The x-axis is drawn at an angle to look like it is coming off the surface. The positive part comes forward, while the negative part goes back. The y-axis replaces the old x-axis, and the z-axis replaces the old y-axis. To graph, start by moving *x* number of spaces along that axis. Then travel **parallel** to the other two axes. Here's an example using the ordered triple (3,-2,4).

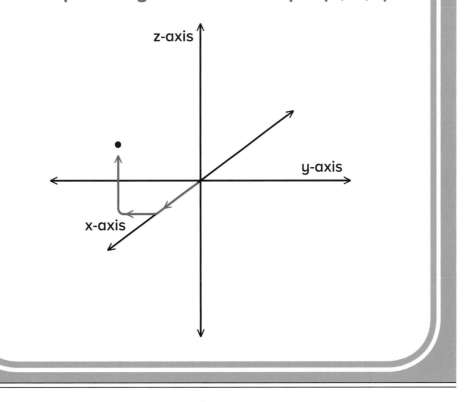

RISE OVER RUN

WHEN YOU CONNECTED TWO POINTS ON THAT GRAPH, YOU MADE A SEGMENT. That segment shows that the relation that generated those endpoints exists for all the other points in between. However, your relation stops at the two endpoints. If you want to show how a function can continue past those points and go forever in either direction, you will need to include arrows. This indicates that the points form a line.

You can blame Euclid, the Greek mathematician and "Father of Geometry," for starting all this discussion of lines and points. Euclid stated that two points determine a line. So if you can generate two

EUCLID COMPILED MANY IDEAS ABOUT MATH IN HIS BOOK CALLED *ELEMENTS*.

points from a function, you can draw a line representing that function.

After graphing a line, mathematicians like to examine the different characteristics of that line. They will often calculate the slope, which is the measurement of how steep a line is. Slope, designated by the variable m, tells how the line behaves. Slope can be positive, where the line goes up as the x-value increases, or negative, where the line goes down as the x-value increases. Slope can also be zero, when a line is horizontal, or undefined, if the line is vertical. A good way to remember these different examples is to picture a winking face.

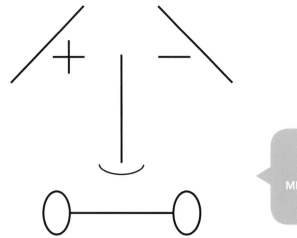

THE "WINKING FACE" SERVES AS A VISUAL MNEMONIC, OR MEMORY AID, FOR SLOPE.

In this winking face, the lines with positive and negative slope are two eyebrows, with the signs of their slope representing the eyes. The vertical line is the nose, while the U-shaped line beneath it means "undefined" and represents the philtrum, the dent under our noses. The horizontal line, which has a slope of 0, represents a mouth with two dimples on each side. Picturing this face can help you remember what type of slope a particular line has.

Being able to identify slope as positive, negative, zero, or undefined is an important skill. However, mathematicians also like to find a value for the slope. Slope is calculated as the **ratio** of the rise to the run (rise/run). The rise is calculated as the change in the y-values of points on the line. The run is the change in x-values. To figure out the slope, first find two points

GPS Locations

Two points determine a line, but in global positioning systems (GPS), three satellites determine a location. A GPS receiver can calculate the distance from a person to a satellite. When that distance, or radius, is known, a **sphere** with that radius is formed around the satellite. The process is repeated for two more satellites. The receiver can then use the intersection of those three spheres to determine location. The location becomes more accurate as more satellites are sighted.

To figure out the SLOPE, FIRST FIND *two points on the graph.*

on the graph. You start at the point that is on the left, and work your way to the right. You always want to approach a math problem in the same order as you're reading this sentence—from left to right!

Count the blocks up or down to find the change in y-values. If you go up, the change in the y-values will be positive. If you go down, the change in y-values will be negative. Working from left to right ensures your run will always be positive. Allowing just one part of the slope to become negative will make reducing the **fraction** much easier.

Take a look at the following example of calculating slope with a graph. First, you will need to pick two points. If you choose points that lie on the grid lines, you will have two whole numbers in the ordered pair. Count up from the first point to get to the level of the second point. That number will be the rise, and it goes in the numerator (top) of the slope fraction. Finish by counting the number of blocks from left to right to find the run, which goes in the denominator (bottom).

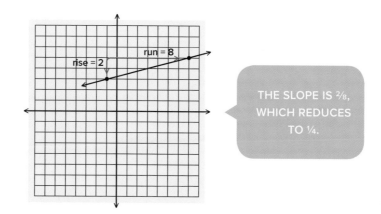

rise = 2
run = 8

THE SLOPE IS ⅔,
WHICH REDUCES
TO ¼.

Although having a graph is handy, it isn't necessary for finding slope. There is a formula you can use, too. All you need to do is substitute the values from the ordered pairs in the correct places. If the first ordered pair is (x_1, y_1) and the second ordered pair is (x_2, y_2), then the formula would look like this: $m = (y_2 - y_1)/(x_2 - x_1)$.

But how do you use this formula? Read through the following example to find out.

Find the slope between these points: (-1, 3) and (7, 5)

x_1	y_1	x_2	y_2	**Label each point with (x_1, y_1) and (x_2, y_2).**

$m = (y_2 - y_1)/(x_2 - x_1)$ — **Copy down the formula.**

$m = (5 - 3)/(7 - -1)$ — **Substitute the values.**

$m = (5 - 3)/(7 + 1)$ — **Any time you subtract a negative value, make sure it changes to a plus.**

$m = 2/8$ — **Do the calculations for the numerator and the denominator separately.**

$m = 1/4$ — **Simplify your fraction by putting it into lowest terms.**

Calculate the slope between the pairs of points in the exercise below. To help you remember the steps to take, a list has been provided.

1. **Label the ordered pairs (x_1, y_1) and (x_2, y_2).**
2. **Substitute into the formula.**
3. **Change any subtraction of a negative number into addition.**
4. **Calculate for the numerator and denominator.**
5. **Reduce the fraction into lowest terms. Always leave slope as an improper fraction.**

(4, -1) and (1, 8)   **(1, 2) and (3, 8)**   **(-3, 5) and (4, -2)** *

Answer Key: Problem D

In addition to slope, mathematicians also examine the intercepts of a graph. An intercept is the place on the graph where the line crosses over an axis. The ordered pairs of these points have one coordinate that is equal to zero. The x-intercept is an ordered pair $(x, 0)$ where the y-value is zero. The y-intercept is an ordered pair $(0, y)$ where the x-value is zero.

To calculate the intercepts of a graph, substitute zero for the other variable. (If you wanted to calculate the x-intercept, you would substitute zero for y.) See how this works in the following exercise based on the graph represented by $y = 4x + 8$.

x-intercept:	$0 = 4x + 8$	Substitute zero for y.
	-8 -8	Subtract eight from both sides to get x by itself.
	$-8 = 4x$	Simplify.
	$\div 4 \div 4$	Divide both sides by four.
	$-2 = x$	Simplify.

The x-intercept is -2, which means the graph crosses the x-axis at -2. The ordered pair for the x-intercept is (-2, 0).

To find the y-intercept, follow a similar procedure.

y-intercept:	$y = 4(0) + 8$	Substitute zero for x.
	$y = 0 + 8$	Any number multiplied by zero is zero.
	$y = 8$	Simplify.

The y-intercept is 8, which means the graph crosses the y-axis at 8. The ordered pair for the y-intercept is (0, 8).

Mathematicians assign a special letter to the value of y in the y-intercept. They call that value b. The y-intercept is an important value for lines, especially when it comes to actually drawing the graph for an equation of a line. Most equations for a line are written with y by itself on one side of the equation. A generic equation like this is in the form $y = mx + b$, where m is the slope and *b* is the y-value for the y-intercept. This is called slope-inter-cept form because it is easy to identify both the slope and the y-intercept.

The graph of any line can be drawn from the equation. In order to draw a graph, you just need a starting point. After that, you can use the slope to generate more points. Read through the following example to see the process in action.

EXAMPLE:

y = ⅓ x - 2

The y-intercept is -2: the value of *b* in the equation will give the y-intercept. Use the operation in front of the number to determine whether *b* is positive or negative. Since 2 is being subtracted, the y-intercept is -2. To start your graph, move down two on the y-axis. Plot a point in this place.

The slope is ⅓: this means that, to move from one point on the graph to another, you need to go up one and to the right three. Then you can plot another point.

Because you need only two points to draw a line, you could put down a straightedge, or ruler, and connect those points. However, if there is space on your graph, try and put down a couple more points so that your line can be as accurate as possible.

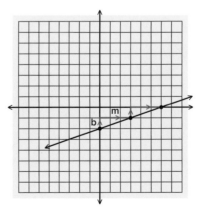

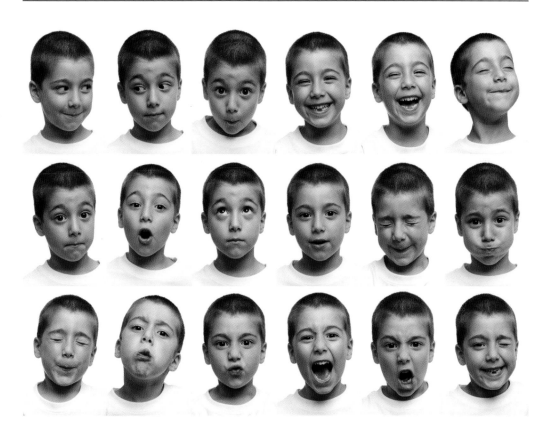

Now try graphing the following equations of lines. Start by finding a point, and then move to the next point by using the slope. If the slope is not in fraction form, put a one in the denominator to make the run equal to one. For example, a slope of four can be thought of as ⁴⁄₁.

$$y = 4x - 3 \qquad y = {}^{-2}\!/_3\, x + 4 \qquad y = {}^4\!/_3\, x - 2 \quad *$$

Being able to work with lines by calculating their slopes and drawing their graphs is an important skill. Any situation involving the relationship between two variables can be represented with a line, including many real-world situations. For example, the cost of a cell phone bill is related to the amount of data used. In addition, slope does not go away as you do harder math. In fact, it becomes a more complex subject as you get older. Just wait until you get to **calculus**!

*Answer Key: Problem E

GRAPHS THAT AREN'T STRAIGHT LINES

APART FROM LINES, MATHEMATICIANS GRAPH OTHER FUNCTIONS SUCH AS QUADRATICS (X^2) AND CUBICS (X^3). Many of those graphs represent more real-world situations. Imagine playing catch with some friends in physical education class. How do you know that the ball will get to your friend in time for her to catch it? You can't throw the ball straight up in the air, unless your friend is right next to you. If you throw it at too low of an angle, it still won't make it. You have to throw it at the perfect angle so that it arcs down to your friend in exactly the right place for her to catch it.

The ball follows sort of an upside-down U as it travels through the air. In fact, all projectiles follow a similar arc. If you want to see how this works, get up and try a standing long jump. In a standing long jump, the goal is to jump as far forward as you can without making a running start. When you jump, when are you at your highest point? What is the path your body makes in the air? It should follow an arc similar to the one the ball would take as you

THE PATH THAT A PROJECTILE (SUCH AS A BASEBALL) TAKES IS CALLED TRAJECTORY.

threw it to your friends.

Mathematicians call this U shape a parabola. A parabola is a mathematical way of representing the flight of a projectile through the air. It is the graph of a quadratic function, and it is a different curve from the curve of the arc of a circle. A quadratic function is an equation whose input is squared. If x is the input, a quadratic function is one where x^2 shows up. This means that x is multiplied by itself. For example, when $x = 2$, $x^2 = 2^2 = 4$.

Depending on the function, a parabola can either open up or down. Any positive number in front of the x^2 term makes a graph that looks like a U. For example, $y = x^2 + 4$ will be a graph that looks like a U. However, $y = -x^2 + 4$ will open down, making an inverted U. The quadratic equation that can be used to model the flight of a ball would have a negative sign in front of the x^2.

Predict whether the graphs of the following quadratic equations will open up or down. (Making an accurate guess will help you double-check your graph later.)

$$y = 3x^2 - 7 \qquad y = -4x^2 + 1 \qquad y = -\tfrac{1}{2}x^2 + 8 \text{ *}$$

To help you draw a graph of a quadratic function, first make a table of ordered pairs. Let's do an example for the function $y = x^2$. When you are trying to pick points for future graphs, remember to pick both positive and negative numbers. You can start by picking five points, but if you don't have enough to make the other half of the U shape, then you may have to choose more numbers.

*Answer Key: Problem F

FIGURE IT OUT!

Equating Motion

When you throw a baseball, it travels horizontally as well as up and down. Using math to describe the ball's path requires some calculus, but the quadratic $y = \frac{1}{2} gt^2 + v_0 t + y_0$ determines the height (h) at any time (t). The many variables in this equation help describe what is happening in reality. The pull of **gravity** (g) is -9.8 m/s². The velocity, or speed, of the ball as you let go is v_0, and the initial height, the spot from which the ball is released, is y_0. This is the basic equation for projectile motion.

Remember to follow PEMDAS as you calculate the other value. Solve for the exponents before multiplying any other values. If there is a number to multiply with x^2, make sure you square the input first! This is especially important with negative numbers, which, when squared, will always equal positive numbers.

Table 1

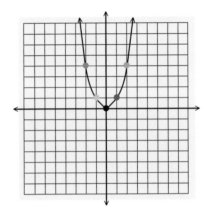

x	$y = x^2$	(x, y)
-2	4	(-2, 4)
-1	1	(-1, 1)
0	0	(0, 0)
1	1	(1, 1)
2	4	(2, 4)

This graph of $y = x^2$ is called the parent function for quadratics. As the parent function, it is the most basic function and graph. Any other quadratic you can think of is a variation on that original function. For example, quadratic equations can also include an extra x term that is not being squared. In fact, even though $y = x^2$ is the parent function for quadratics, the standard way they are written is $y = ax^2 + bx + c$. The letters a and b are coefficients, or numbers that multiply variables.

The function $y = 2x^2 + x - 4$ is an example of a quadratic written in this way. When you start adding in those different operations, order of operations becomes very important. To keep track of everything that you are calculating, it is beneficial to add an extra column to the table to show your work, as done in Table 2. The total in that column for each input represents the output, or y-value. Before you graph $y = 2x^2 + x - 4$, you will first square the input for x. Then multiply that new number by two, add the value of x, and finally subtract four from that sum, as shown in Table 2.

Order of operations BECOMES VERY *important.*

Table 2

x	2x² + x - 4	y	(x, y)
-2	2(-2)² + (-2) - 4 2(4) + (-2) - 4 8 + -2 - 4 = 2	2	(-2, 2)
-1	2(-1)² + (-1) - 4 2(1) + (-1) - 4 2 + -1 - 4 = -3	-3	(-1, -3)
0	2(0)² + (0) - 4 2(0) + (0) - 4 0 + 0 - 4 = -4	-4	(0, -4)
1	2(1)² + (1) - 4 2(1) + (1) - 4 2 + 1 - 4 = -1	-1	(1, -1)
2	2(2)² + (2) - 4 2(4) + (2) - 4 8 + 2 - 4 = 6	6	(2, 6)

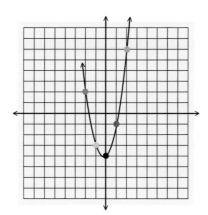

Now it's your turn to try graphing the following equations. Begin by creating a table to generate points.

$$y = -2x^2 + 1 \qquad\qquad y = x^2 + 2x - 4 \text{ *}$$

Answer Key: Problem G

You can graph ANY EQUATION *you are given*

Being able to generate ordered pairs through the use of a table is a great skill to have. If you can master this, you can graph any equation that you are given. You can do quadratics, where x is squared. You can also graph a cubic function, where a number is multiplied by itself three times. The following exercise shows how to deal with an x^3. The product, or answer to a multiplication problem, of two negative numbers is a positive number, as you saw when you squared them. However, the product of three negative numbers will equal a negative number.

Table 3

$y = x^3 + 2$

x	x³ + 2	y	(x, y)
-2	$(-2)^3 + 2$ (-2)(-2)(-2) + 2 -8 + 2 = -6	-6	(-2, -6)
-1	$(-1)^3 + 2$ (-1)(-1)(-1) + 2 -1 + 2 = 1	1	(-1, 1)
0	$(0)^3 + 2$ (0)(0)(0) + 2 0 + 2 = 2	2	(0, 2)
1	$(1)^3 + 2$ (1)(1)(1) + 2 1 + 2 = 3	3	(1, 3)
2	$(-2)^3 + 2$ (2)(2)(2) + 2 8 + 2 = 10	10	(2, 10)

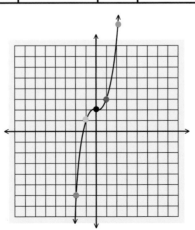

Try graphing the following cubic equations on your own. Be sure to fill in a table and include a column for showing work. That extra step may save you some headaches if something goes wrong and you have to re-trace your steps. Everyone makes mistakes, but the people who show their work are able to find and fix their mistakes more easily!

$$y = x^3 + 5 \qquad\qquad y = -2x^3 + 1 \ *$$

Being able to make a table to generate ordered pairs for a function will help you graph anything! Ordered pairs are the first things that you learn to graph. Once you have mastered those, it makes all graphs easy to draw. Practicing your calculations with inputs to find outputs will also help you do graphical math. Those inputs and outputs then can easily be represented on a coordinate plane, thanks to the work of Descartes, Fermat—and you!

That extra step may save YOU SOME HEADACHES if something goes wrong

*Answer Key: Problem H

MATH TOOLKIT

1. While versions of calculators have existed for more than 450 years, graphing calculators were not developed until the late 1900s. Casio introduced the first, the fx-7000G, in 1985. Five years later, Texas Instruments entered the market with the TI-81. Both calculators could graph many mathematical functions, but the TI-81 could store more functions. Since then, the graphing calculator market has exploded. For example, Texas Instruments now has models with full keyboards and color graphs.

2. A graph's range, which can be determined from the equation, will tell us just how high a graph will climb. A graph that has a range of infinity will continue forever. But graphs with a specific range flatten out at a certain point. When this happens, they approach asymptotes, lines that act as invisible barriers. The graph on the left will continue forever. The graph on the right approaches the asymptote and will not go any farther.

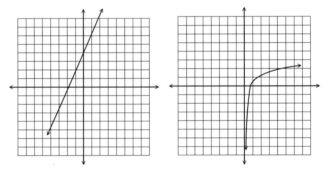

3. Although you can graph any equation that is in slope-intercept form by using those two parts (slope and intercept), the graphs of horizontal and vertical lines are approached in a different way. The acronym HOYVUX can help you when working with these lines.

Horizontal lines have a slope of **O** (zero) and their equation is written **Y** = the value of the y-intercept

Vertical lines have a slope of **U** (undefined) and their equation is written **X** = the value of the x-intercept

4. The largest exponent in an equation tells the degree, which determines the graph's shape. Graphs with an even degree (2) will have U shapes. Graphs with an odd degree (3) will make S curves. The degree affects the number of turns a graph makes: that number is always one less than the degree. The graph of a cubic, for example, turns twice. Knowing the graph's shape and its number of turns will help you check the accuracy of your graph.

GLOSSARY

acronym: an abbreviation made by the first letters of other words

algebra: a branch of mathematics that uses letters and numbers to solve for unknown values in different equations

calculations: operations performed on numbers

calculus: a branch of mathematics that studies change, usually on an infinitely small level

coordinate plane: a flat surface made up of the x-axis, y-axis, and four quadrants used for plotting points

equations: math sentences that connect two equal expressions, which are combinations of numbers, variables, and operations

fraction: a number that relates pieces of a whole quantity by division

geometry: a branch of mathematics that works with the properties of shapes

gravity: the force that pulls two objects to one another; on Earth, its acceleration is given as the quantity $g = -9.8$ m/s^2 ; the value is negative because gravity pulls objects down

improper fraction: a fraction in which the numerator is larger than the denominator

lowest terms: describing fractions whose numerators and denominators do not have any factors in common

number theory: a branch of mathematics that studies the properties of numbers, especially positive numbers

operations: procedures performed on numbers, such as addition, subtraction, multiplication, or division

parallel: describing lines or paths that will never cross

powers: numbers that have been raised to an exponent

ratio: a comparison of two quantities through division

sphere: all points in space that are the same distance from a given point

two-dimensional: existing with only length and width, like a flat surface

variables: letters that are used to represent unknown quantities

SELECTED BIBLIOGRAPHY

Berlinghoff, William P., and Fernando Q. Gouvêa. *Math through the Ages: A Gentle History for Teachers and Others.* Washington, D.C.: MAA Service Center, 2004.

Dilke, O. A. W. *Mathematics and Measurement.* London: British Museum Press, 1987.

"How does GPS work?" Physics.org. Accessed June 21, 2014. http://www.physics.org/article-questions.asp?id=55.

Rooney, Anne. *The Story of Mathematics.* London: Arcturus, 2008.

Struik, Dirk J. *A Concise History of Mathematics.* New York: Dover, 1987.

Woerner, Joerg. *Datamath Calculator Museum.* Last modified June 24, 2014. http://www.datamath.org/.

WEBSITES

Circus Classroom: Projectile Motion
http://www.pbs.org/opb/circus/classroom/circus-physics/projectile-motion/
This website explains projectile motion through the use of juggling.

Desmos Graphing Calculator
https://www.desmos.com/calculator
Practice using an online graphing calculator on this site.

Note: Every effort has been made to ensure that the websites listed above are suitable for children, that they have educational value, and that they contain no inappropriate material. However, because of the nature of the Internet, it is impossible to guarantee that these sites will remain active indefinitely or that their contents will not be altered.

INDEX

ANSWER KEY

Problem A

E (1, 6)   F (-2, -2)   G (-5, 3)   H (6, -2)

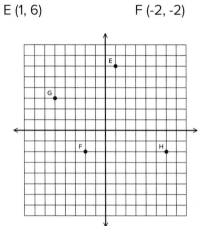

Problem B

J (4, -3): in Quadrant IV

K (-1, 7): in Quadrant II

L (-6, -5): in Quadrant III

M (0, 3): not in a quadrant, on the y-axis

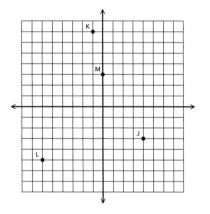

Problem C

y = 2x + 7:

y = 2x + 7	y = 2x + 7	y = 2x + 7	y = 2x + 7
y = 2(1) + 7	y= 2(2) + 7	y = 2(3) + 7	y = 2(4) + 7
y = 2 + 7	y = 4 + 7	y = 6 + 7	y = 8 + 7
y = 9	y = 11	y = 13	y = 15
(1, 9)	(2, 11)	(3, 13)	(4, 15)

y = 5x - 2:

y = 5x - 2	y = 5x - 2	y = 5x - 2	y = 5x - 2
y = 5(1) - 2	y = 5(2) - 2	y = 5(3) - 2	y = 5(4) - 2
y = 5 - 2	y = 10 - 2	y = 15 - 2	y = 20 - 2
y = 3	y = 8	y = 13	y = 18
(1, 3)	(2, 8)	(3, 13)	(4, 18)

y = -4x + 6:

y = -4x + 6	y = -4x + 6	y = -4x + 6	y = -4x + 6
y = -4(1) + 6	y = -4(2) + 6	y = -4(3) + 6	y = -4(4) + 6
y = -4 + 6	y = -8 + 6	y= -12 + 6	y = -16 + 6
y = 2	y = -2	y = -6	y = -10
(1, 2)	(2, -2)	(3, -6)	(4, -10)

Problem D

(4, -1) and (1, 8):   (4, -1) and (1, 8)
x_1 y_1 x_2 y_2

$m = (y_2 - y_1)/(x_2 - x_1)$
$m = (8 - -1)/(1 - 4)$
$m = (8 + 1)/(1 - 4)$
$m = 9/(-3)$
$m = -3$

(1, 2) and (3, 8):   (1, 2) and (3, 8)
x_1 y_1 x_2 y_2

$m = (y_2 - y_1)/(x_2 - x_1)$
$m = (8 - 2)/(3 - 1)$
$m = 6/2$
$m = 3$

(-3, 5) and (4, -2):   (-3, 5) and (4, -2)
x_1 y_1 x_2 y_2

$m = (y_2 - y_1)/(x_2 - x_1)$
$m = (-2 - 5)/(4 - -3)$
$m = (-2 - 5)/(4 + 3)$
$m = (-7)/7$
$m = -1$

Problem E

y = 4x - 3:   m = 4 = 4/1, b = -3

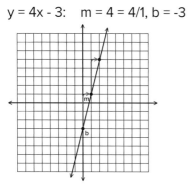

y = -²⁄₃ x + 4:   m = (-2)/3, b = 4

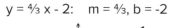

y = ⁴⁄₃ x - 2:   m = ⁴⁄₃, b = -2

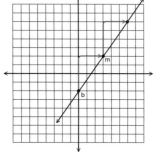

Problem F

y = 3x² - 7: opens up

y = -4x² + 1: opens down

y = -½ x² + 8: opens down

Problem G

$y = -2x^2 + 1$

x	$y = x^2$	(x, y)
-2	4	(-2, 4)
-1	1	(-1, 1)
0	0	(0, 0)
1	1	(1, 1)
2	4	(2, 4)

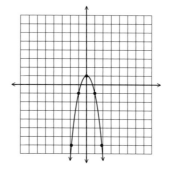

$y = x^2 + 2x - 4$

x	$2x^2 + x - 4$	y	(x, y)
-2	$2(-2)^2 + (-2) - 4$ $2(4) + (-2) - 4$ $8 + -2 - 4 = 2$	2	(-2, 2)
-1	$2(-1)^2 + (-1) - 4$ $2(1) + (-1) - 4$ $2 + -1 - 4 = -3$	-3	(-1, -3)
0	$2(0)^2 + (0) - 4$ $2(0) + (0) - 4$ $0 + 0 - 4 = -4$	-4	(0, -4)
1	$2(1)^2 + (1) - 4$ $2(1) + (1) - 4$ $2 + 1 - 4 = -1$	-1	(1, -1)
2	$2(2)^2 + (2) - 4$ $2(4) + (2) - 4$ $8 + 2 - 4 = 6$	6	(2, 6)

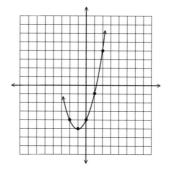

Problem H

x	x³ + 5	y	(x, y)
-2	(-2)³+ 5 (-2)(-2)(-2) + 5 -8 + 5 = -3	-3	(-2, -3)
-1	(-1)³+ 5 (-1)(-1)(-1) + 5 -1 + 5 = 4	4	(-1, -4)
0	(0)³+ 5 (0)(0)(0) + 5 0 + 5 = 5	5	(0, 5)
1	(1)³+ 5 (1)(1)(1) + 5 1 + 5 = 6	6	(1, 6)
2	(2)³+ 5 (2)(2)(2) + 5 8 + 5 = 13	13	(2, 13)

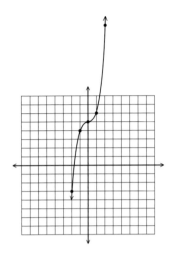

x	-2x³ + 1	y	(x, y)
-2	(-2)³ + 5 (-2)(-2)(-2) + 5 -8 + 5 = -3	-3	(-2, 17)
-1	(-1)³ + 5 (-1)(-1)(-1) + 5 -1 + 5 = 4	4	(-1, -3)
0	(0)³ + 5 (0)(0)(0) + 5 0 + 5 = 5	5	(0, 1)
1	(1)³ + 5 (1)(1)(1) + 5 1 + 5 = 6	6	(1, -1)
2	(2)³ + 5 (2)(2)(2) + 5 8 + 5 = 13	13	(2, -15)

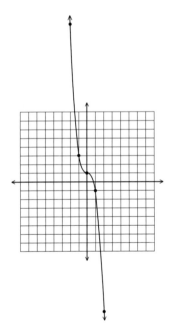